Finding Strength in
Our Scars

Kaylin Floyd

BookLeaf
Publishing
India | USA | UK

Finding Strength In Our Scars © 2023
Kaylin Floyd

All rights reserved.

No part of this publication may be
reproduced, stored in a retrieval system, or
transmitted, in any form or by any means,
electronic, mechanical, photocopying,
recording or otherwise, without the prior
written permission of the presenters.

Kaylin Floyd asserts the moral right to be
identified as the author of this work.

Presentation by *BookLeaf Publishing*

Web: www.bookleafpub.com

E-mail: info@bookleafpub.com

ISBN: 9789358310245

First edition 2023

My Rainbow

I hate that I get sad
Because I know I've been through worse
But it still hurts so bad
It feels like I'm forever cursed

This reoccurring pain in my heart
Feels like it's being ripped apart

I don't want to feel this way anymore
My eyes are getting sore
From the constant tears shed
You'd think nothing was left unsaid

But quite the opposite

Constantly pushing my feelings down
You would never know my smile was really a
frown
To the point where it's now an overflowing pool
of emotions
I just can't control it

You see emotions are like colors of the rainbow
All blending into each other

Making it difficult to tell where one ends and
where another begins

And as my emotions spill over
My rainbow blends into shades I've never seen
before

And those who see this mess
Come rushing like I'm a damsel in distress
Poking and prodding
Trying to figure out what's wrong with me

But no matter what I say
They never really understand

And now this feels like a chore
Explaining over and over again
But what for
It'll never be the answer they're looking for

So for now I'll just close this door.

Me

Growing up in a predominantly white
neighborhood
You don't see many people who look like me
I'm one out of the three
That stands out on the playground

And when the kids come around
They'd look at me and ask
"What are you supposed to be?"

And because I didn't match anyone's skin tone
they had seen
They couldn't identify me

I couldn't identify me.

Growing up watching the screen
I never saw one of me
No one I could look up to and say
Wow, she looks like me

A biracial woman.

Who struggled to see where she fit in
Because of the color of her skin

Because she never blended in
To the crowd that society only allowed

African American, Caucasian.. Which are you?

I wondered that too
What to check off on my college application
That tells me to choose

Picking one or another
Still feels like I lose
So I choose the box other

But who said you can put me in a box?
The one society just wants me to check off

Who said you can tell me, I'm not black enough
Not white enough

Why even care about this stuff?

You made me feel like I was living in two
worlds I didn't fully belong in
2 identities that never collided

So as a young girl, I was misguided
By the lies and judgement of others

But now that I'm older

I wish I could have told her

That she's beautiful just the way she is
Don't listen to those kids

And the next time someone asks "What are you
supposed to be?"

Just tell them I am Me.

Wounds

My dad left when I was 18
And it felt like my whole world fell apart
I was lost in a pool of memories
That I felt were forever gone

And as my wounds began to heal
My memories felt alive again
I couldn't ever bear to feel
The way I did back then

But the more people I meet
The harder it becomes
To not grieve those who stay for only a chapter

My whole world shatters

And here I am again
Lost in a pool of memories
My wounds ripped open

I'm stuck here
Alone
Drowning in this ocean

Does it ever get any easier?

Because I'm just so tired

Tired of my heart breaking
Tired of my world shaking

I wish things were different
But I know it's not permanent

My wounds will become scars
And my heart will disregard
All the pain it endured

For a minute
I feel reassured
That this feeling won't hurt as bad
The next time I feel sad

That I'll be stronger
I'll last longer

But my wounds are so deeply woven into me
They've become a part of me

Holding me tightly
Like I do with those in my life

And letting someone go is like losing a part of
me
And it feels like I won't survive.

The World vs Me

Why is it that I feel trapped
In a world that wants me to adapt
When all it does is stab me in the back?

Falling from a participant to an observer
I had to nurture the emotions of a 12-year-old
girl

Who wished only one thing in this world
To be accepted.

To be accepted for who I am
And not see the world like the boogeyman.

So afraid of the world as it is
What more could I give?

Giving too much of me
Was a scary and vulnerable thing
And I feared the world would bite back at me

Little did I know, my inner self bit harder.

I don't know who I was more afraid of

The world or the inner girl who acted as a
martyr.

I wake everyday to a lump in my throat
As my inner self fights to stay afloat

Fights to be heard
And tries to reassure me that it is ok to be who I
am

But I swallow her down
Thinking I'm protecting her from the world's
playground

I don't understand why she fights me
Aren't we living a good life?
Ya sure, we might think twice about every
decision
And never roll the dice

But we're safe
And if we stay silent, no one can hurt us.

So I stayed silent
Watching my life go by from my window
But as time grew, that silence mocked me

Surrounded by four walls
All I have is the quiet to keep me company

I suddenly miss that inner girl who used to leave
a lump in my throat
If you come back, I promise I will help you stay
afloat

Because this loneliness is scarier than anything
And now I realize I am missing everything!

I thought looking through my window
Vicariously through others
Would keep us from feeling small

Well, I was wrong
I'm only 12 after all

I realize now it wasn't the world that was against
me
I was against me.

Moving on

I feel so empty now that you're gone
But I see everyone around me has moved on
As if you were never here
And that's my biggest fear

Moving on

Because doing that feels like I'm putting you on
a shelf
And that feeling hurts more than anything else

You see all my memories are stored on these
shelves
And the longer they sit, the easier they become
to forget

And I'm scared

Scared that you'll become a distant memory
That it'll feel like you were never real
And I won't feel the way I used to feel

About you

About us

And I can't even discuss
What a life like that could be

Because you see

It feels like I don't know a world without you
And it's crazy because now I have to

But the reality is
I lived a life without you
For so long
I can't even remember how I was so strong

But now that you're here, I can't seem to let you
go
And now this familiar sadness starts to overflow

My heart starts to ache
And the tears roll down my face

And I want to sit in this feeling forever
And replay the memories we made together

But I should know better
That I have to get myself together

But if I let myself be ok
And let the pain go away

Then that means I'm ok without you
And I don't want to be.

My Childhood home

I stand here
Looking at the outside of a house that I don't
recognize
And all my eyes can do is criticize
Because all I see is a house that's disguised

What once was composed with life and color
Is now masked with somber and a color gray as
ash

I peek across the fence
With a high amount of suspense
In hopes to see my childhood home once again.

I can still hear the echoes of laughter in the walls
The quick-paced footsteps of my siblings
running down the hall

The sensation of comfort in the rooms
And the smell of BBQ in the afternoons

And as I continue to reminisce
That sense of bliss disperses
And immerses with anger

Because what we left there, they can now call theirs
All the new repairs my parents spent years doing

When a dream house is what they were pursuing

Well, they got that dream house
But it was taken away from us too soon

Forced to leave, only taking what we could carry
While the rest was left to be buried

I mourn over what couldn't be carried
I mourn a house that made us merry
If you haven't realized yet this is an obituary

I mourn over what got left behind
And what I used to be able to call mine

This is the funeral of my childhood home.

So yes when I look over that fence
All the great memories do come rushing back again

But when I look over that fence
And see they get to have what we made at our expense

I get a sense of pain and sorrow
Because I know neither today nor tomorrow
Will I ever get to step foot in my childhood
home again.

I'm okay

I'd never thought I'd be ok without you
But here I am
Standing on two feet

Here I am
Swimming in an ocean full of memories
I used to drown in

Here I am
Putting the last puzzle piece of my shattered
world back together again

You know I cried for days after you left
I barely slept

And writing these poems about you gave me a
sense of peace
But these are ones you'll never read

Because these were for me
For me to see

That I don't have to keep pushing my feelings
down
When people come around

That I don't have to watch my rainbow bleed
over
And lose composure

Because I found something that helped me get
through you leaving

Something that won't keep me in these feelings.

And now it feels like I'll survive
I put the ignition in drive

And look out at the landscapes as I pass them by
Reminiscing in the memories we had

And I don't cry

I smile.

Thirty, Flirty and Thriving

At 13 years old I already pictured my future
where I was an adult

Didn't we all?

Wanting so fast to see the results
That looking to the future became an impulse

"Thirty, flirty and thriving"
Filled with hunger
Becoming an adult seemed so appetizing

I thought I was over all the hobbies and the
games
Ready to replace them with a blazer and a
briefcase

Not knowing that as an adult I was going to have
to face
The regret of moving life at such a fast pace.

It's funny as children we want so badly to be
treated like adults
And once we become one, we wish to go back

Back to the day where our only worry was what
to eat for a snack
And where all I should have wanted was a cute
top and a backpack.

Life as an adult is not what I expected

And not because of all the bills and
responsibilities
But because I'm disconnected

Disconnected to the 13-year-old me
To the girl who loved to try new things
And was excited of what life would bring

I don't know where she is now, but I will find
her.

Broken

I feel broken.

Literally I'm broken.

My body can't keep up with my fast pace and
rigorous lifestyle
Which only consists of me going to work, going
to the gym and typing on a computer

The list goes:

Groin injury, plantar fasciitis
Voice condition and tendinitis

Dealing with one thing after another
It feels like I'll never recover

It's so frustrating
Debilitating

To see my friends move forward in life
While I'm stuck here waiting
For the doctor to arrive

I guess this is my life

Watching my health decline
And feeling envious of my friends who are fine

But this doesn't define me
It can't

And after hearing myself rant
I am not going to allow my injuries to define
who I am

I am a warrior
Strong and resilient

And I won't concede in this fight
Because I know I'll win it

It's time I take control of my life
And strive to live it

Because in the end
I'm the only one who can rebuild it.

Hopeless Romantic

To be loved by someone
Is something we all want

A love that will knock you off your feet
And will make your heart skip a beat

Handwritten letters
And kissing in the rain

I can feel your love written all over the page

A sunset with a picnic
Riding horses on the beach

Holding hands with you was always so sweet

I guess you can tell I'm a hopeless romantic
Wanting things that might never even happen

Well, let me tell you

Fictional characters have ruined my love life
The idea of a perfect person has been ingrained
since childhood

It's caused me to be picky as hell
Waiting for the right person
I guess the 'perfect' person
To come my way

Wanting romantic dates straight out of the
movies
Is something that's consumed me

Someone bring my head out of the clouds please
Because I don't know what to say

I love "Love"
And I can't stop fantasizing about meet-cutes

Men in suits

And all the I love you's

I know someday I will find my person
Not some fictional character from the movies
But someone real.

Finding Me

Sometimes having a near-death experience
Reminds us to live life to the fullest

Without that, we get so caught up in trying to
make a living for ourselves
That we forget to have fun along the way

While my near-death experience happened when
I was 17
It was the year 2020 that changed things for me

Everything that I loved got taken away from me
All my hopes and dreams
Of what my future could be

And that truly scared me

Because while I never sought to reach those
dreams
All I wanted to do was scream

Because all those opportunities were gone
I would prolong and prolong
I don't even remember why I waited so long

Fear.

Fear is why I waited so long.

Fear is always around the corner
Full of body armor
Ready to take over

Fear is the reason why we're always in
off-season
Fear is the reason why we're only dreaming.

I flashback back to the 13-year-old me
Who wasn't afraid of anything
And was excited for what life would bring

I want that girl again
And only then, will I win this fight.

Flash forward to 2021
I am that girl again

The girl who loves trying new things
And has big dreams

Who now loves finding new hobbies
And embodies the woman that I want to be

I am so lucky
To have found me.

Just Breathe

"Just breathe", they say
As I sit here crying in pain

"All I do is hear you complain"

So confused by the situation
I'm the only one that they can blame.

"Just breathe", they say

Oh, I know how breathing works

I inhale, the air enters my lungs
I exhale, the air leaves my lungs

If I could
Don't you think that I would?

"This is your fault Kaylin."

"What did you do to yourself?"

"This doesn't make any sense to me."

Blaming.. blaming.. blaming..

This is all I heard.

Words become blurred
Everything sounds so absurd
And now my mind is obscured
Covered by a fog of hurtful words

The only thing that was clear
Was the growing fear
Rotting in my stomach

The fear that I would have to update them on my
situation
And hear the frustration in their voices

"It doesn't make any sense to me."

"Why can't you just breathe?"

Right then, I knew
That I was going to have to go through this
alone

If only this could be postponed
So they had time to understand what they don't
know.

I can hope and pray all I want
But I'm still alone

A voice in the wilderness
Calling out into an empty space
And no one can hear it
Or is it that they just won't listen?

What changes between a child and an adult
Where we stop believing in things we can't see?
And this might be me reaching
But I can't put my finger on it

Do we just stop believing in things we don't
see?

Do we not believe in the wind because we can't
see it?

But we can feel it.....

Can't we?

We believe it, because we feel it.

And I know you can't see my pain
But I sure as hell can feel it

I feel the jabbing in my throat

The dryness that makes me start to choke
The taste of metallic
You think this is a joke

I'm sinking on this ship alone
Can't you hear it in my tone?
I need help, please help me
Please throw me a life jacket
Because I can't do this alone!

I have never felt this low.
I now know what it's like to hit rock bottom.

I can only go up from here right?
That's the saying everyone says

So I tried
I tried my hardest to get myself out of rock
bottom

I went to therapy
And I know they're just doing their job
But this was the first time I heard someone say
I understand, I hear you
I don't know what pain you are feeling, but I
hear you

And I just cried and felt relief
Because someone finally heard me

To say those words to me meant everything
It meant I wasn't fully alone.

And soon later on everyone finally understood
what was going on
But it was too late
Because my pain was already gone.

Gone too soon

Death
Is a hard concept to understand.

It's not the uncertainty of reaching the promised
land
But the fact that someone could just slip out of
your hands
And be gone

Forever.

A grandfather whose laugh would light up a
room
And an uncle who loved to play with his nieces
and nephews

Both slipped out of my hands
And left this world too soon

To go back up to the stars with God
While I'm left here on earth
Replaying each memory of them over and over
again

What we used to do for fun

What I wish we could have done

What I wish we should have done.

Over and over again they play
But nothing can be undone
And what I wish won't be enough

I'm trying to comprehend
But my mind loves playing tricks on me
Imagining it's them I see
Waving in the doorway as I drive up to their
home

Because I hate to see my grandma alone
I hate to see my mother come home
To her empty brothers' room
Wondering why God had him leave so soon

Death is a hard concept to understand.

I'm still trying to comprehend
And come to terms with the fact
That my loved ones are never coming back
again.

Mirror

I look in the reflection, and what do I see?
Chubby face, chubby thighs and Bug Bunny's
teeth

Why do I so hardly criticize
What my big brown eyes see?

I guess it's hard not to
In a world where beauty standards say, you
should be a size 3

Magazine cover captions: "World's most
Beautiful Women and their Secrets to staying
Fit"

But the one thing that they omit
Is how much they edit their bodies to look
skinny and fit

And now young girls are idolizing a body that's
not realistic
And it shows in the statistics
That mental health issues are at an all-time high

Because society loves to lie

Just to get us to buy
Products that claim to get us to that ideal body
type

It's sad
That these magazines make women feel so bad

So what I want you to do, is grab a pen and
notepad
And write down three things you love about
your body

I'll go first:

I like my eyes, my big brown eyes
Don't apologize if you're mesmerized

I like my butt
Makes me want to go out and strut

And I like my legs
Not tall enough to get out on the runway
But I can rock a dress any day

This is a reminder that you are beautiful just the
way you are.

You don't need a magazine to tell you what you
should be.

Because the most important thing is that
You love you for you and I love me for me.

The Queen and the Jester

I see the way you look at me
Like picking the best apple from the tree

Looking to find the sweetest one
One that won't cause you trouble
And can get you a home run

You see you think you're the king
And that you can overrule me
Because in your eyes I'm the jester
Here to entertain thee

But what you were too distracted to see
Is that I am actually the queen

So I'm sorry that I've intervened your routine
Of picking apples from your tree.

Women are not some delicious snack
That you can take and devour
Throw away when you're bored
Or when it gets sour

I believe chivalry is not dead
That there are still men who instead

Treat women with respect

Who wants to connect
Rather than select
A random apple
That they choose to neglect

A man who will love and care for me
And not just want to fuck me

A man who will be honest
And promise they won't run when there's
conflict

So get this straight in your head
So that you won't ever forget

I'm a mother fucking queen
So treat me with some respect

Perfection

Born the oldest out of three
It was an exciting thing to see
All my siblings looking up to me

But I didn't know the responsibilities
That came with paving the way

As I got older
I soon understood the term
Monkey see, Monkey do

And I knew I had to choose
How I do and what I do wisely

If they were in trouble
I was troubled
Because I felt the pressure
To continue to be the positive role model

And it started to feel awful.

Feeling watched not only by my siblings
But now by parents of my friends

Who always bumped heads

And wished they were more like their friend

"Kaylin is the perfect child"

"Why can't you be more like her"

I would have preferred
If they didn't say a word
At least not in front of me
Don't you think?

Because now I can't make any mistakes
Both at home and when I walk out the door.

You know this isn't something I asked for.

These high expectations
Come with unwanted attention

And now you've created the foundation
Of a girl who knows only perfection.

The Phoenix

Before if you asked me if I was excited about
life
I would've told you no

Little did you know
My mind was stuck in a chamber
Filled with sorrow and darkness

Trying to light a match was pointless
As it wasn't enough to see through the dullness

You see I had gone through so much turmoil that
I felt hopeless
I had lost focus
And I'm sure people noticed

Hindered by this darkness, I lost who I was in
this process
And it took me a while to address how much I
was depressed

My depression was a roller coaster
One minute I could let my arms hang free
And the next I was grasping the bar tightly
My head down in my knees

Next to me, was a dusted matchbox
Cobwebbed and gray
For so long it had laid

I had almost forgotten about it
I didn't have the will then
But, what if this time
I tried again

So I struck the match
And the darkness thinned out and dispersed like
a puff of smoke

The warm sun glistened on my face
And I was now ready to embrace the life that I
used to be excited for

It was a long journey to get here
But nonetheless, this is the premiere
Of the girl that has risen from the ashes.

My Nemesis

Tonight is the night
Where I'm expected to live up to your high
expectations

With my breath shaky
And my mind hazy
I'm hoping this kind of pressure doesn't break
me

The circus tent packed with a rowdy audience
Leaves me feeling less and less confident

"All I have to do is get to the other side"

As a tightrope walker
This requires attention and focus

But in a second everything felt hopeless
Because what I didn't notice
Was the rowdy audience was actually my inner
critic

And as I tried to cross the rope
They shouted all my negative thoughts

"You can't do it"

"You are not good enough"

"You'll never reach your full potential"

Such powerful thoughts
I had no doubt in my mind I was going to fall.

We are our hardest critics
And it is only ourselves who don't allow us to
succeed

And it is ourselves who hurt us the most.

And I was this close to believing those lies
My inner critic tries to disguise as the truth

There is a fine line between disappointment and
expectations
And while I always try to strive for greatness
I've hurt the person who believed in me the
most.

I don't know how to fix this
Me being my own nemesis

But for now all I can do
Is try my best to be attentive and focused

As I walk across the tightrope.

Spoken Words

Poetry: A literary work in which special
intensity is given to the expression of feelings
and ideas

A quality of beauty and intensity of emotions

Words that were spoken from my heart
And from places in me that are very very dark

I found poetry when I had my recent heartbreak.

From a boy who was never mine
But could have been mine
If we only tried
Before you left

I can't sleep
I wake at 3 am

My heart hurts
And I don't know where to begin
To start healing

I can hear my heart breaking
And feel a sadness I've never felt

And all I felt compelled to do was write

Write what I was feeling
What I was dreaming
Until I realized what I was writing was a poem

Writing every night I had gotten in the flow
Of pouring my heart out on paper

Something that was new and exciting
And was providing a therapeutic aspect to my
broken heart

I could feel the heaviness in my chest leave
As I started to unweave
The thick vines caged in my heart

This was the start of me letting go of what
wasn't meant to be
And what would set my heart free

Thank you for finding me
And coming into my life at a time
Where I was feeling broken

Because now I found a community of friends
Who can see through my lens
And allow me to express
The deepest parts of who I am.

My Journey

We are on a journey through life
Each on our own path
Looking through our own eyes

And sometimes our eyes peer over at other lives
Which causes us to undermine
Where we're at in our life

Envious of others
What they have
What I don't have

What they got
And what I want

And now I'm looking at my glass
Half empty
And not half full.

But life is not a race
And each journey goes at their own pace

My journey right now might not be about
finding love

The kind of true love many around me have
found

The love I have been searching so hard for
That it almost felt like a chore
Is maybe not the door I need to open right now

At this moment in time, my journey might not
be what I want it to be
But what it needs to be

Maybe
It's self-love that I need
To love more of me

To learn who I am
To love who I am
To be proud of who I am

Maybe this journey is about Me.

Strength in Our Scars

Life is a journey for all of us
There will always be ups and downs
And we will always face trials

But we always tend to dwell
On the downs in life

The struggle, the pain

It's tattooed on me
For everyone to see

Constantly living in my present
I knew it was there to torment
Every decision I made

Each scar reopening
As I'm reminded
Why I can't do this
Or why I can't do that

It's hard to accept my present situation at times
I spend so much time fighting my past
Sometimes I feel paralyzed

Constantly thinking a situation should never
have happened
When I should have been coming to terms with
the fact that it did happen.

Our present situations exist from a long chain of
events
That started far in our past
And being angry won't improve my future.

I have a lot of scars on my body
Some that may last
And others that have stayed in my past

But each scar holds a story
Gets put in a category

Mostly containing hardship and sorrow
And ending with the question of
How can I get through tomorrow?

I'm shedding tears
For what felt like years
And having these scars was a hard pill to
swallow

But as I look back and reflect on these scars
There's a girl still standing
Despite what they've caused

So I am proud to show those scars tattooed on
my body.

Because the girl right here, right now
Is stronger than she's ever been
With all the trials she's been faced with

I no longer want to look at my past
And become attached to all the wrongs
I wish to make right

This is my life
And I choose to strive
And walk the streets with pride

Because my scars are not a sign of weakness
My scars are my strength.

Printed in the USA
CPSIA information can be obtained
at www.ICGtesting.com
LVHW011247130324
774240LV00014B/873

9 789358 310245